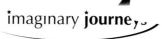

IMAGINE ON

24 fun ways to picture and tell marvellous stories

Rob Parkinson

Book 2 in the series "Natural Storytelling"
Published by Imaginary Journeys
27 London Road, Tonbridge, Kent TN10 3AB UK
Tel/fax +44 (0) 1732 362356
E-mail: info@imaginaryjourneys.co.uk

www.imaginaryjourneys.co.uk

First published November 2005
© Rob Parkinson 2005

IJ202

ISBN - 0 - 9549001-1-1

1.

IMAGINE ON

Contents

INTRODUCTION

If you have been on a journey, then you have a story to tell
(Trad. saying)

Imagine On is the second in a series of four booklets, each of which explores a different side of story making and telling through fun oral techniques. These are ways of working I've used in hundreds of workshops with both children and adults over more than twenty years as a professional teller of tales and workshop leader.

Everyone imagines. It's a natural human faculty - and a very essential and central one at that. Without it, there would be no language, no art, no science and no entertainment for a start. But not all of us use imagination in the same ways, nor do we do so well or consistently. Using imagination is a skill like any other; it responds to practice.

In *Imagine On*, the focus is on the use of natural imagination. You could call it the dreaming mind, the 'inner storyteller' that dominates in dreams and fantasies. All good teaching starts from what we can do naturally – and dreaming and fantasizing does come naturally. But in story making and telling, it needs to be both triggered and focused.

The techniques here all work around multi-sensory picturing – not just seeing in imagination but hearing, tasting, feeling, touching. You could call it guided imagery for creative purposes if you want a grand sounding title. The most common way of thinking about imagination is visual – making pictures in the mind's eye. Many people who visualize in this sense may regard themselves as imaginative. However, imagination is making mental images, not just 'scenes' – representing to ourselves in whatever ways are, as it were, thrown up by the brain/mind. There are people who represent inwardly mostly through modes other than sight and it's important to remember this when working with participants of any age in workshops. Various tips to help in making allowances for different imagining styles are given in the introduction to Part 1 and elsewhere.

Whilst the presentation here may suggest work with children of primary school age, most of the ideas can be used as a basis for working with teenagers and adults as well. Again, suggestions are given in the notes. Many can also be made to work with the younger infant and even pre-school children, though as anyone who is familiar with young children knows, you have to simplify a lot, adapting creatively. For very young children, imagination is very real and scarcely distinguishable from every day reality; effective story work subtly gives them ways of reality testing and beginning to control imagination as well as stimulating it.

The booklet is divided into two parts, each of which has its own separate introduction. The second section, in which the picturings in the first are developed through some oral games, is much shorter, but the games explained in other books can also be used with the picturings. And in any case, picturers can always just tell the stories imagination has shown them in whatever ways emerge, without any formal artifice.

As in other books in the series, techniques and games are accompanied by notes under three headings:-

General note: In this category, there are a few points about the origins of the imagery etc. However, the focus is largely practical - how you can make the idea work best, how it can be simplified or extended, how it might be adapted to suit different ages groups, which other techniques in this and other books it can be linked to and so on.

Story skills: Points here cover some ideas specifically about story and language coming out of each technique. There is only space for hints - many more ideas will come out of imaginative exploration. But teachers in schools will want to connect to practical 'measurable' story skills in the current target-driven education climate, so the notes are to assist in seeing those connections. In

4.

more relaxed workshop situations and in one-to-one interactions, the story skills can be allowed to emerge naturally.

Interesting: Here I've given a few suggestions about an equally important element in many story techniques, which will be useful to anyone using those in the present volume in emotional education or indeed in therapy, healing and healthcare. Stories connect very closely with personal meaning; it is not really possible to hive off any extended work around story as being only for creativity or entertainment or language development, especially work that seeks to really engage the imaginative mind. It's hence better to be aware of the many concomitant powers a picturing and a story can have and to use those powers positively as and when it is both possible and necessary. Readers who would like to understand this much better are referred to my book *Lantern of Imaginings* (HG Publishing, Spring 2006).

Imagination is a truly marvellous faculty. It's a sad shame to see the natural imaginative faculties of so many bright young people spurned so readily in favour of the deadening, off-the-shelf, commercially-driven fantasy of the media. The effects each one of is capable of producing in the portable home-theatre of imagination are very largely beyond the budgets of even the richest film moguls. And what's more, imagination is free - and what is even more, it can yield real personal treasures. That alone should be reason enough for using and developing these simple fantasy picturings with a modicum of respect - mixed with a large dash of fun.

Rob Parkinson, November 2005

PART 1. IMAGINE IT

This section presents a series of eighteen multi-sensory picturings. These can be used alone as starting points for stories both oral and written. It's also possible to link games as is suggested in the notes and illustrated in Part 2, where you'll find various ways of developing the picturings in fun oral games. They are set out in an approximate order, progressing from simpler picturings stressing only the positive to more complex, shaded imaginings. Many of the picturings are culled from the landscape of traditional myth and fairy tale, but they can all be adapted to more contemporary settings with just a little extra imagination..

PICTURING

There are many ways to enhance the effectiveness of the picturings. Here are some brief tips:

1. Circumstance and preparation: It's easier to imagine when there are fewer external distractions. Talking through a few priming ideas and then doing very short imagining exercises (purple horse galloping; a bright orange sky with turquoise mountains and silver palaces; sighing breeze in trees; smell of fresh-baked bread/coffee etc.) helps to prepare the way for more extended picturing.

2. Eyes: Whilst it's good to close eyes and focus inwards, many can imagine well with eyes open. However, with children an eyes-closed rule restricts mutual distraction.

3. Using sound: Focusing on a sound such as a bell or gong for a minute or so is one way to create the right kind of stillness. Children can be challenged to notice how long the sound lasts. If you have skill on an instrument, this can also be helpful.

4. Give most instructions indirectly: Where possible, ask questions and make open suggestions rather than insisting, giving options about what to imagine rather than commanding.

5. Make it multi-sensory: Whilst 'picturing' suggests making visual images inside the mind, imagination can work equally through other senses. By using words that invoke sight, sound, taste, touch, feeling (both emotional and bodily-kinesthetic), you can cater for all styles of imagining. Think of ways to evoke each sense.

6. Speak slowly and leave long gaps for imagining.

7. Encourage concentration obliquely: Groups often respond better to imagining if challenged – 'You just couldn't imagine ...' 'You'd never be able to stay quiet and just concentrate on the pictures...' or even paradoxically 'Don't imagine this...' – listeners somehow ignore the 'don't'

8. Improvise on the skeleton - spin out parts of the picturing to draw listeners deeper into the imagining, asking more questions etc.

Developments: The images given here should inspire further picturings. Traditional stories, are a very rich source of ideas and images, as is more modern fantasy and science fiction - and indeed mundane-seeming ordinary life. As familiarity develops, workshop group members may enjoy making up picturings and presenting them to the group themselves. As will become clearer, the current set of picturings have a family resemblance, so that there is the potential to use them together in making a longer quest tale.

Scenario & stages: The picturings are set out with a paragraph to set the scene, followed by a series of questions to indicate possible stages. Although these could just be read out carefully, it's usually better to adjust the wording and formats given, which are intended as rough guides. Picturings can be done all the way through, or interrupted at any (or each) stage to feed back and tell stories about what has been 'seen'. It's also possible to use these stages with primary age children as directions for acting out in dramatic improvisations and through movement and dance.

1. THE FANTASY ROOM

Scenario: This is your chance to design a room of your own, a very special fantasy room in which you could spend hours and even days and weeks. You can have in it, by means of its magic powers, almost anything you like to make it particularly comforting and safe and soothing. But there is no TV or radio or computer or telephone in the room and you will go there completely alone to begin with, because it is a very private place just for you. It can have magic windows through which you can see what you want to see when you want to see; you can add to it in whatever other ways you like – remember that it is magic. It is up to you how the room develops.

Stages:

1. As you open the door to this room, you can begin to get a clearer idea of it. What do you notice first as you go into it? What feelings do you have?

2. What sort of walls and floors and doors and windows will there be? How many doors and how many windows? What is the ceiling like? What colours and patterns and scents and sounds will you allow in this room? How does the air you breathe there taste?

3. Can you see through any of the windows now and, if so, what kinds of view do you have?

4. What feelings tell you that this room is particularly yours and particularly safe and comforting?

5. What are the first extras you would like to add to this special room and how do they look and feel as you imagine them?

6. You can put in this room all kinds of good times and good feelings you've had in the past as well as good feelings you want to have in the future. What else will you do to the room to make it even better and especially your own. (You can list these to yourself.)

7. How often would you like to go into this room and what new things could you start to do there?

8. How much of the story of this special room will you tell and how will you tell it?

General Note: *Young picturers can be daunted by the no TV etc./no people rule, but with encouragement, this picturing sets up a secure imaginary base for further imagining work. Invoking the room can be a shortcut to reaching a relaxed, focused state from which the other picturings can start. And these might, for example, be 'seen through the windows' of this room, whilst the room itself can be encouraged to go on growing and developing with each visit, as imagining skill grows. Picturers can go on to share parts of the picturing they want to reveal in No. 19 I Witness or No.20 Whisperings.*

Story Skills: *Story making and telling becomes really interesting when the teller/writer realizes just this kind of freedom to make things as they wish. The room tells a very personal story, not all of which picturers may wish to share – which is again the kind of decision any story maker or teller has to make.*

Interesting: *Quite similar images are used by some relaxation teachers, meditators, therapists - and indeed by sports coaches and performers. This is partly because they allow people to draw on and focus their resources imaginatively. Imaginative work on a special room can improve confidence and a sense of self-security, done in the right way. Description of such imagined rooms can also at times be usefully revealing.*

2. THE GOLDEN STAIRCASE & THE MAGIC DOOR

Scenario: Somewhere (indoors or outdoors) where you feel particularly relaxed and confident, a beautiful golden staircase appears, suddenly and apparently by magic. It looks fascinating and you can go along it (up or down, however your imagination wants it to be). At the end of the staircase (top or bottom), there is a door with a key and a handle, both ready for turning. The door can be opened and on the other side will be something wonderful, which you'll soon be able to see and sense very clearly. You can go through the door for a short time if you wish. You'll then return along the golden staircase, When you step off it, it will disappear though you can always find it again.

Stages:

1. You could enjoy the happy feeling of being in the relaxing place – it could be the Fantasy Room or somewhere connected to it.

2. What is it that is so attractive and interesting about the golden staircase? Perhaps there are patterns, or shapes or some mysterious sound.

3. How does it feel as you move along the staircase? Do you float along evenly or go by stages? Can you see the door to begin with or is it hazy and vague?

4. As you get closer to the door, you can start to see it more clearly. Maybe there are pictures or carvings or strange patterns and colours. It might feel pleasantly warm and there could be incredible scents. Can you take a closer look at the key and the handle before opening the door?

5. Some people see the marvellous something that is beyond the door immediately and others take more time and watch it emerge slowly. You can take your time to notice a few details. Do you want to go through the door and sense more vividly for a moment or two or would you prefer just to look?

6. How will it feel as you close the door and return along the staircase? How will you notice that the staircase disappears as you leave it ? Can you sense how you are able to bring it back when you need to?

7. What things will you put into your story of the Golden Staircase and the Magic Door?

General note: The staircase image may not suit all people – for example, very obviously anyone wheelchair-bound. It is possible, however, to substitute chair lifts, elevators etc. and have the same effect. Notice that optimistic feelings are stressed throughout. Whilst some will balk at the freedom in this visualization and want more direction, by repeated practice of exercises like this, it's possible to discover the pleasures of making use of free imagination.

Story Skills: This is another starting point visualization that can be complete in itself or lead on to a more developed story. Inspiration is a vital element in story making often overlooked. If the tellers can be persuaded to really imagine their way beyond the door, there is a motivation for making a story inspired by this (though note that 'something wonderful' has no very clear meaning). If they can't, it doesn't matter because they can talk and write about the given elements of the staircase and the door.

Interesting: Optimism is very powerful. Optimistic people have in general been found to actually live longer with less illness and healthier lives. This exercise, done in the right way, can be a practice for the skill of optimistic imagining.

3. CLOUD 9

Scenario: You will be able to float on the legendary Cloud 9. This is a cloud people normally get to ride upon when they have won a million pounds or have discovered that their true love loves them or won a big race. But this ride can just happen. The cloud floats up to you when you are somewhere you like very much – perhaps in the Fantasy Room. You can sit or lie or stand in it and enjoy the feeling of floating up and away and beyond and looking back at the things your normally do. Maybe you can even learn to control the cloud in some ways, so that it will take you where you want to go.

Stages:

1. Where are you just before Cloud 9 arrives? What kinds of feelings and sensations tell you that you like being in this place?

2. What does Cloud 9 look like? How does it feel as you touch it? Does any music play as you climb onto it?

3. This cloud has a silver lining so is entirely safe. What is the feeling of relaxing even more deeply inside the cloud? Do you notice how it rises up and goes way up into the air?

4. What sort of view do you have when you look back from the cloud? Can you see your home and places you would normally go to?

5. Can you find ways to control that cloud and take it to particular places you choose? Maybe you would like to drift around weightlessly for a while.

6. How will you return from the cloud to the place from which you started?

7. How will you tell the story of a ride on Cloud 9?

General note: *With children (and with adults too with a little inventiveness and/or cheek), this can be offered as a challenge – 'Here is something you just won't be able to imagine, because it's much too difficult.... 'No one has ever ridden on a cloud so you can't possibly imagine it...' Storytelling afterwards can be much easier if picturers are asked to mentally mark and record experiences, perhaps by checking off (say) three things about the cloud/sensation/view etc. on three fingers – which also makes a memory training exercise. The cloud can become a vehicle to lead into other visualizations – for example,* No 4. The Castle in the Air.

Story Skills: *Telling the story of this imaginative experience demands use of all kinds of language about the senses to give a clear impression of how it felt and looked etc. It's possible to focus on, for example, how legs and arms felt as the teller relaxed into the cloud or what kind of things/colours/landscapes etc. were seen from a distance. Similes should occur very naturally – because the imaginative experience is created using similitudes. 'It's like...' can be picked up on and developed more artistically.*

Interesting: *Floating on the cloud is another optimistic, 'can-do' image and is also useful for 'distancing'. For example, supposing a group or individual is nervous or apprehensive about a forthcoming event, taking them beyond the*

Fantasy Room and up on Cloud 9 where things can be seen in perspective can allow them to gain a perspective, especially if it is suggested that it all looks a much smaller and less important from the cloud.

4. THE CASTLE IN THE AIR

Scenario: People talk about building castles in the air as if it meant only day dreaming, but now is your chance to go to just such a castle. You can visit this strange and unusual place and find there whatever your imagination wants to show you. There may be treasures or thrones or knights or fine ladies or dragons or griffins or unicorns and all sorts more. It all belongs to your imagination, so you can make it the way you would like it. Anything you don't want to stay in the castle can be sent away to the far horizons.

Stages:

1. How will you get to the cloud? Will you use Cloud 9 or perhaps the Magic Carpet (No.8) or some mythical flying beast you have tamed (see No.7)?

2. Seeing the Castle in the Air from a distance, what do you notice about it? Do you see colours and particular shapes or hear music? What things would you like to tell another person about this amazing sight?

3. As you approach and enter the castle, perhaps you can notice how easy it is to go inside? Are there gates or doors to open? Is the castle empty or are there magical servants waiting to help and to obey?

4. What is the first really important and interesting thing or place or person you see inside this castle?

5. Is there a large hall or other big room? Do you climb up towers or go down flights of stairs as you explore the castle? What kinds of things do you find as you investigate?

6. Are there are any things you would now like to dismiss from this castle? (If you like, you can do that now and watch them become distant dots away on the horizon.)

7.Are there any things you would like to bring into the castle or any other changes you would like to make? (If so, you can allow your imagination to make these very clear.)

8. Does the castle have some special secret, known only to you?

9.How will you rule over this castle and what will you do there? Will you be able to come and go to this castle as you choose or do you want just to leave it now?

10.How will you tell the story of this castle and which things will you mention first? Which things might you keep secret or only tell to close friends?

General Note: *More detailed and extended imagining is being asked for here. The castle is a more formal structure than a cloud - there are outer parts like walls and gates and towers and turrets to note and inner parts like halls and high rooms. The fantasy of this place may take many different directions. Incidentally, the 'castle in the air' need not be a castle at all – older picturers might prefer to do it as* Magical Mansions *or* Perfect Pavilions *or any image that allows them to fantasize in more modern ways.*

Story Skills: *Creating the castle in imagination is like the work of the story maker and teller in creating an imaginary world so believable that it becomes real. Also, thinking through in advance the kind of detail to be included in the telling of a tale makes that telling work better.*

Interesting: *The kind of day dreaming that is referred to as building castles in the air is healthy in many ways, kept within limits. For example, it indicates that a person has hope and interest in alternative futures – and that is something of which both children and adults who have been through difficult times can lose sight. This picturing can be a substitute and a rehearsal for spontaneous day dreaming with anyone who has lost touch with that natural skill. Because it is optimistic, it can again encourage optimism.*

5. THREE MAGIC GIFTS

Scenario: Somewhere (perhaps in the Castle in the Air, perhaps at the top of the Golden Staircase beyond the Magic Door) you will find a chest. Inside this are magic gifts – caps of invisibility, swords of sharpness, potions that give super strength or extraordinary beauty, rings of power or knowledge, magic mirrors that show you anything you wish to see, magic bags and boxes and all sorts more. You may look at as many of these as you wish, but you can only take away three of them. None of the gifts is all powerful, so you won't get endless wishes or power that can't be bettered; the powers of each gift can be great, but always limited. To get each magic gift, you must spend some time imagining it clearly, making sure you can say at least three things about it. The more things you can say, the more powerful it will be when you take it away.

Stages

1. You may like to spend a while relaxing in the Fantasy Room or floating on Cloud 9 before finding the chest. Perhaps you'll go up the Golden Staircase and open the Magic Door.

2. Where is the chest and what does it look like? You can spend a few moments looking at it, noticing its shape and size and smell and feel.

3. How will you open the chest? Does it have a key and is it easy to open or does it take a little extra effort?

4. Because it is magic, this chest can hold enormous things as well as tiny ones. Which gifts will you notice first and how are all these incredible things arranged inside the chest? You can look at as many gifts as you wish before choosing...

5. It is time to make your first choice. Look at Gift 1 carefully, hold it and sniff it in your imagination. Notice at least three things you can remember about it and mark them by counting through three of your fingers.

6. Going on to your second choice, again you can spend time imagining it in the same way, making sure you have it clearly recorded with at least three things to say.

7. Now you can do the same with your third choice.

8. Check back through all three gifts and see if you can imagine them all together in some way. List on your fingers again the things you will say.

9. How will you tell the story of getting three gifts, the way you found them and how you closed the chest and came home or went on travels, the ways you will use the gifts.

General note: *Magic gifts are common in fairy tale and myth as well as in more modern fantasy literature and it should be possible to list many examples in advance through discussion etc. It's important to stress the 'not all powerful' rule, especially if this picturing is to be followed eventually by Terrible Trials as suggested (p.46 etc.). Again the fantasy/ fairy tale setting is not essential to the use of the game - magic powers can be replaced by extraordinary abilities, skills and talents to make a game that works well with teenagers for example. Novice picturers/story makers may like to start with just one gift – it takes memory skill as well as imagining to recall all three gifts.*

Story Skills: *The Rule of Three in story structuring and elaboration is explored further in* Book 3. Spinning the Yarn. *and* Book 4. New Lamps for Old, *but is important in many of these picturings. Three details are usually enough to build a picture in description – this way of building up pictures can be explored separately. Three gifts are the usual complement and often connect to a tripartite adventure of some kind, so that this picturing readily links to the use of traditional plots.*

Interesting: *Picturers who are particularly needy in the psychological sense can metaphorically connect the gift/ability etc. in the picturing with what they lack and would like to acquire. This can happen unconsciously. In appropriate circumstances, this linking can be exploited to their benefit – for example, a person who lacks confidence and is self conscious can imaginatively use an instrument of power like a sword or wear the cap of invisibility, symbolically rehearsing confident, unselfconscious action.*

6. THREE MAGIC HELPERS

Scenario: You are going to meet three magic helpers. None of them will be all-powerful, so that they cannot grant any and all wishes, nor make you completely unbeatable etc. Each will have one particular range of skills — carrying you through the air at great speed, fighting fierce enemies, making marvellous houses instantly, drinking whole seas and so on. They might appear human or be mythical beasts or animals or strange creatures. They will be very friendly. When you have imagined them very clearly, you can take them back to your ordinary life or perhaps go on a quest or other adventure with them. The more clearly you imagine them, the more powers they may have, so you will be able to say at least three things about them (and up to seven).

Stages:

1. You can start from the Fantasy Room, go floating on Cloud 9, go up the Golden Staircase, enter the Castle in the Air or whatever you choose. Where will you go to meet the helpers? Can you make a mental picture and describe the place to yourself in your own way?
2. How will the first helpers arrive or show him/herself etc.? What do you notice first about this helper? Does the helper demonstrate the powers he or she has? What tells you that you can trust the helper, who will always do what you say? Will the first helper stay with you or will you be able to summon him or her up in some way?
3. Can you think of at least three things you will be able to say about the helper, so that other people can get a feel for what he or she is like? (You might like to think of size, the clothes he or she wears or the fur if it is an animal, the feeling he or she gives you etc as well as the strange power.)
4. How does the second helper arrive or show him/herself? Go through all the questions and ideas listed under 2 & 3 to help you get a clear image.
5. Now do the same thing with the third magic helper.
6. You can imagine all three helpers together in some way and notice how they obey your commands.

7. What challenges and difficulties do you think each will help you in facing? Will they stay with you in some way or must they leave you once they have helped?

8. How will you tell the story of finding the three helpers? Can you imagine an adventure in which they will help you and bring you safely home at last?

General Note: *Another popular motif in fairy tale and legend, so again it should be easy to list possibilities. This is an alternative or a complement to Three Magic Gifts (No.5), which it resembles, though now the magic comes from helpers who might become companions in ordinary life happenings (as for example in the Heroes, Heroines & Fools storytelling game p.45) or in a quest or other extraordinary adventure (see Terrible Trials p.46 or Heart's Desire p.24). Magic helpers can also be compared (and even combined) with games in* Book 1. Tall Tale Telling *such as* Peculiar People *(No.12) or* My Friend Boogle *(No.17). Again, novice storytellers may start with one helper. Again it's possible to leave the traditional fantasy world and have especially skilled/talented servants, coaches, champions etc.*

Story Skills: *Once more descriptive powers are developed using the Rule of Three, this time with a living being of some kind. Once more memory in oral telling is challenged. Stories developing out of the picturing illustrate how tales can be shaped around aspects of character – what the helpers are able to do will link with what they actually do as part of the story, whilst three events in which they may be involved give a story basic shape.*

Interesting: *Similar remarks to those made under Three Gifts apply. As in many traditional stories, the helpers can represent aspects of self to be discovered and utilised. The advantage with an imaginary being as opposed to a fantasy artefact is that it can have a character and a voice. Many people have found simple ways to use imaginary helpers in everyday life, particularly with children. One parent, obliged to give a child regular injections, created stories with her around a marvellous flying lion that could carry away pain.*

7. TAMING THE FANTASY STEED

Scenario: You can have an exciting and extraordinary ride on a fantasy 'steed'. This can be anything from a flying horses or a unicorn, a dragon, a talking tiger or a giant eagle to a supersonic motorbike or an aerobatic car. However, you will have to tame the steed first. It is not easy to approach, let alone to mount and ride. The tiger might be fierce, the motorbike seems to have a mind of its own. You will have to use a mixture of patience and cunning and perhaps a little knowledge. You will have to tame the steed and get to know it before you can ride it. Then you can have that ride.

Stages

1. You can spend a while in the Fantasy Room, looking at a few moving pictures of possible steeds and reading up on them before you make a choice. There are a lot of possibilities...

2. What sounds tell you that your Fantasy Steed is arriving? Where will it be when you see it first? What tells you that it won't be easy to do that taming?

3. What sort of plan will you make for taming that steed? Will you offer it some sort of food or will you play it sweet music? Think through the plan before doing anything.

4. Can you imagine the stages of taming the steed and getting to know it? Can you go through those stages on your fingers. (The more fingers you can use, the more the steed will trust you and do as you say.

5. Now it's time to mount the steed. Can you imagine how you do this, how you will take control?

6. You can get the steed to move forward, but this stage is dangerous. Perhaps you will lose control for a moment or nearly fall off. How will you cope with that and make sure you have full control. What is the feeling of controlling the steed like?

7. Now you can start to really travel at speed. Notice some of the things you see? What makes it an exciting ride? What kinds of places do you pass and where does the steed take you on this first ride?

8. Will there be any dangers and threats to pass and escape from?

9. What will it be like to travel homewards? Will you keep this steed secretly or share it with friends and family? In what other kinds of adventures might the steed be involved?

10. How will you tell the story of the taming of the steed and the marvellous ride? What makes your ride particularly special and how can you explain this?

General note: *The symbolism of riders and mounts is used in all kinds of cultures and crops up in public statuary as well as in all kinds of fantasy literature. This picturing is more demanding than earlier ones where all things and experiences are simply given. Picturers have to work harder to take command and use the mount. Having the steed available can be given special importance in a development game like* Terrible Trials *(No.22) or* Hearts Desire *(No.24) – the well imagined steed can be allowed as an additional gift/helper. My song,* Winston & the Wolves *(Wild Imaginings CD IJ103) is a succinct treatment of the 'taming the mount' theme. Again, the essence of this picturing can be taken out of the mythical/fairy tale setting - the steed can become, say a marvellous guitar or a special outfit.*

Story Skills: *Descriptive and analytical skill is again developed through conveying not only the look and feel of the steed but also the strategy and then the exhilaration of the ride. And again the nature of the 'beast' will naturally connect with the way the plot of a consequential story develops.*

Interesting: *Learning to tame and control the steed can be made metaphorically like learning to tame and control any faculty, skill or talent – like the faculty of imagination itself. A feature of taming and controlling a mount is a degree of trust and freedom allowed to the 'mount' itself so that it can use its powers to good effect.*

8. THE MAGIC CARPET

Scenario: Maybe everyone should have a ride of a magic carpet once in their lives. This one can just arrive one day and there it will be. Once you can see it clearly, you will be able to understand how to use the patterns on it to make it fly. You can then get to know better and better how to command it. After a while, you will be able to go anywhere you choose. To begin with, however, you may have to compromise by thinking of a place and then accepting the way the carpet 'hears' your choice – which will differ from your intention. That can lead to some strange and even silly situations until you learn to get it right.

Stages:

1. You may like to start by making a clear picture of the carpet as it arrives, or you can wait for a while in a relaxing imaginary place and allow it to happen by.
2. As you begin to get a clearer vision of it, how does the carpet look? What sort of textures can you feel? Does it have a smell that you notice? What colours and patterns do you see?
3. It's time to sit on the carpet and take a long and careful close-up look at the patterns and designs... You can notice particularly interesting parts of the pattern and how these fit into the whole design... How do you know or discover how to make it fly?
4. What is the feeling of taking off and then flying? What sorts of things do you see and hear? Can you notice how you gradually work out ways to make it go right and left, up and down and so on? Maybe you can try flying high and low over some weird sights you didn't expect to see.
5. The carpet can hear thoughts and take you to what you seem to want. Try imagining clearly a place you would like to reach, one you would not be able to get to by any ordinary means of transport.
6. The carpet will take you to something like this place, but it won't be as you imagined it. Can you notice some of the differences? Is there something silly or absurd about the difference you could tell someone to make them laugh?

7. You can try imagining and then going to two more places and see if you can get the carpet to 'hear' your imaginings better, so that the place you reach is more the way you wanted it to be. If the results are still silly when you get to the third place, are there ways you could change that?

8. Will you keep the magic carpet and make it part of your ordinary life or perhaps some kind of adventure.

9. What kind of a story will you make about the magic carpet ride?

General note: At first sight, this can seem simply another version of Cloud 9 *or* Taming the Fantasy Steed. *It differs from* Cloud 9 *in calling for more specific attention to detail and control; the operation of the carpet is more complex and the results less predictable. It differs from the steed picturing - the carpet is not a being and it also takes picturers to unexpected places. Magic carpet imagery is usually very fruitful and there are very many other ways to develop it.*

Story skills: The magic carpet makes a very good symbol for the power of fantasy, which in any story work one has to both learn to control but also 'allow to fly'. There are very many possibilities for where the carpet can go. The hint in the sequence here is that there could be a comic element – which is a common feature of brushes with the magical in all sorts of stories.

Interesting: Again the carpet can be metaphorically a faculty or personal power to be understood and developed. Magic carpets can carry picturers away and beyond to new perspectives and can also allow them to focus intentions. The format given here implies also working with idealistic expectation and realistic compromise and seeing some of the humour that could come out of the contrast.

9. THE MAGIC PAINT BRUSH

Scenario: You find or are given a very special paint brush. What you paint with it can be made to come to life as soon as you decide that it is finished. You can experiment with some simple things first to see how that works. Then you might like to tackle something big and ambitious.

Stages:

1. How does the paintbrush come to you? You could spend time flying on the magic carpet before you get this treasure.

2. What does the brush look like? When you pick it up, is it heavy or light?

3. How does a person paint with this brush? Do you have a palette of colours and some water to wash the brush or does it work differently? Do you paint on paper or canvas or on walls or in the air?

4. Maybe you would like to experiment. What would be a simple thing to paint first? Would it just be a line or two that would start to hop around or would it be something quite different?

5. Is there a way of putting aside these first creations – rubbing or painting them out perhaps?

6. You can try something a little more complicated now that you are getting the feel of the brush. You may want to work on the detail before releasing it.

7. Now it's time to try that something big and ambitious. Will you plan out the painting first or just let it develop as you paint it? What colours will you use and what sounds will the brush make as you make that painting?

8. When you have finished the painting, will you have any control over the thing that comes to life or will you let it go?

9. How will you turn the pictures you have been making into a story in words? What will you be saying about the brush and the way in which it works?

10. Can you imagine a person who took a brush just like this one and used it in ordinary life or in the middle of another story?

General Note: The picture that becomes real has had many treatments in children's literature as well as in folk tales and legends. The magic paint brush image can be given a very free treatment if you simply want to liberate imagination. In this outline, there are hints that creation carries with it responsibilities. There is also the interesting dilemma over letting the creation be. The paint brush appears to break the rule given for the magic gifts and helpers – picturers can paint anything, which makes them all powerful. Using the paintbrush in a game like Terrible Trials *(No.22)* can, with a good imagination, make the storyteller more invincible than can, say, magic weapons or armour. Compare this with the Wishes Three *game in* Book 4. New Lamps for Old.

Story Skills: There is a suggested plot to tell here of course, which can be summarized as magic power to create – advantages and disadvantages of this – effect in life of the painter. The exercise is also about how real and effective a story can be made to be, about how much one needs to put into imagining it through and then, perhaps, allowing it to develop according to its own rules.

Interesting: The ease with which a person can create the pictures with the magic brush and then let them go or maintain control may give quite a few hints about personality traits and mental/emotional states. Using the magic brush to fulfil in fantasy all kinds of wishes and dreams can be a very useful and therapeutic exercise. For picturers with emotional difficulties, the power both to create and to erase with the magic brush can be very effective and helpful.

10. SHAPE SHIFTING

Scenario: You are given (or will get or discover) the power of shape shifting. You will be able to change into a different creature as well as being you. This will lead to some adventures. (Later you may also discover how to be two other creatures, though it's best to master the power with just one different shape first.)

Stages:

1. Where does the power of shape shifting come to you? Is it in one of the imaginary places visited in other picturings or somewhere else? Maybe you could find a mental picture of the source or the giver of the power. Do you have to peep into a book of secrets or is a wand waved over you? Do you discover the secret through your own efforts or is it given?

2. You have a choice to make. You can now choose to become any creature. What change will you choose?

3. The change works through careful picturing. You have to get it right in your imagination, so you work through the shape of the creature, getting the main details clear in mind. Once the picturing is complete, then the change can happen quickly.

4. You can practise being the creature and also stepping back into being yourself.

5. Can you imagine being the creature somewhere you know very well – school or work or at home or with friends? What happens? Will this lead to an adventure?

6. Will you find out more about the power and be able to become other creatures? (You could do two more changes in the same way and explore more adventures.) Or will you decide to get rid of the power and if so how?

7. How will you tell the story of the change or changes and the things that happened as a result?

General note: Shape shifting is another familiar traditional motif which has migrated to cartoons etc. The term, however, may need explaining to children, with a discussion about possible changes. Again the ability to change not just to one other being but to three is a theme in many folktales; in the format above, doing three changes is possible, though it is simpler and more effective to do just one initially. Adventures coming out of shape shifting make a good tall tale for use in some of the Book 1 games. The theme is explored with comic effect in my spoof grunge rock song for children, Pandora's Potion *on the* Wild Imaginings *CD (IJ103).*

Story Skills: *Actors talk about 'getting inside the skin' of a character. This picturing takes this quite literally – and empathy is a vital story making and telling faculty as well as an acting skill. Vivid description of what it is like to become and be the other creature(s) and also to become oneself again can be encouraged and will give real interest to the telling.*

Interesting: *The exercise calls for a change of shape, not in essential being though, in doing the exercise, many picturers find themselves naturally taking on something of the character and feeling of the creature whose form they borrow. This can be used for effective insight and even behaviour change, with shy, retiring picturers being asked to become say lions or leopards or over brash and loud types becoming quiet harvest mice. One young girl I know regularly acted the part of a lion to overcome fears of darkness on the stairs at night.*

11. THE MIRACLE MARKET

Scenario: At the Miracle Market you can buy miracles. For example, there are ways of making rocks into cakes, bringing stone statues to life and all sorts of other marvellous possibilities. The difficulty is to decide what to buy, not to get distracted and to see your way clearly to what you want. You have three golden coins of the miracle currency to spend. Really big miracles will cost all three, but you could get three different small miracles. It's best to just look and see what really appeals. Sometimes what looks like junk turns out to be truly marvellous

Stages:

1. What does the miracle market look and feel like? What sorts of sounds can

you hear? Are there rich smells of miracle food and miracle perfumes? Can you see many people crowding around the stalls?

2. You can look at several stalls and notice some wonders? Are there any magic potions, cures for ills, methods for walking on water? Are there some real surprises you'd never have guessed would be there?

3. Can you feel those miracle coins? Do you have a feeling for how you'd like to spend them? You could always take yourself off to the Fantasy Room or stop time whilst you float on Cloud 9 before you make a decision.

4. What will you look for first and how long will it take you to find it? Will it be a really big miracle so that you have to spend all three coins, or a small miracle that costs just one. Where will it be? Can you touch and feel it and notice any shapes

5. If you are looking for a second and third smaller miracle, where will you find those and what will they be like. What else can you see as you leave the market.

6. When you have left the market behind, what will you do with the miracles you have bought? Can you imagine the experience of using your miracle(s) in detail, so that you can really notice their effect?

7. Can you tell the story of each miracle – the getting of it and the using of it and all that happened after that?

General note: The setting of the market can be spun out with many more questions and suggestions, perhaps including one or two strange sights – people on stilts as tall as mountains, vanishings, sudden appearances etc. Miracles can be interpreted as differing in many ways from plain magic, which makes this not the same as Three Magic Gifts *(No.5). And because the bustle of a market can be confusing, there is a good chance that what emerges can be surprising. The suggestion under 3 of using the Fantasy Room is optional and could be kept in reserve for possible use at any stage when picturers need more time. Questioning games like* I Witness *(No.19) or games from* Book 1. Tall Tale Telling *can be used to develop the story afterwards.*

Story Skills: The 'serendipity principle' used in many creative writing and story making classes comes into play in this picturing - random imagining of wonders and strange sights can be encouraged before the coins are spent. Again the use of three coins to make three choices (or one big choice) gives a central plot which will naturally be played out in events imagined after the market.

Interesting: Many people are, of course, covertly looking for miracles. Imagining through actually finding one can be at the least instructive and at best magically effective. This is so because fantasy is not weightless – when you imagine something very vividly, physical and emotional responses can be triggered automatically just as if the imagined thing had happened. This principle can be used very effectively to help with some concerns and is explained much more thoroughly in my book, Lantern of Imaginings *(HG Publishing).*

12. THE PALACE OF POSSIBILITY

Scenario: In the Palace of Possibility there are some astonishing things. It can be even more exciting and interesting than places like the Castle in the Air or the Golden Staircase and the Magic Door, because there can be absolutely anything, including things that are beyond your wildest dreams. But that means that there are also dangers. When you go into the palace, you will need to learn quickly which doors you should open and which to keep locked. When you have learned that, you will become King or Queen of Possibility for the day and rule over the whole palace.

Stages:

1. It's good to take a long look at the Palace of Possibility from the outside first. This could help you to know something about how it works and will be very useful in telling the story of it later. As usual, notice at least three things about the palace you could say to give your picture to someone else through words.

2. The path to the palace passes through a landscape which you will have to imagine for yourself, since the palace is different for every person imagining it... Are there trees or rocks or open spaces, gardens and flowers or dusty deserts?

3. It's time to go through the great door to the palace. Is it easy to open that door or difficult? Does someone open it for you perhaps?

4. The palace could be confusing at first, because there can be so many colours and scents and sounds but, if you look carefully, you might see some patterns or designs that look familiar. You can very safely look around the first part of the palace, where there are some extremely interesting and delightful things to find for anyone who uses enough imagination.

5. There are very many closed doors in this palace. Perhaps they are arranged along corridors, perhaps they are set out in some other way. Somewhere also there are keys to open those doors. Can you imagine how you will find those keys? You could hold them and notice how they feel? Do they jingle or make some other noise?

6. With these keys, you can open any door. But as you look at the doors, how will you know which to open? Is there some way of telling from the outside which are the good doors, which are the bad ones? Is it possible to take a peep through the keyhole first? Do you notice some kind of pattern of colour or sign on the best doors?.

7. What happens when you open a good door? Can you notice some fascinating experiences you'll have there and some ways you can mark that door for opening again when you want to?

8. What happens when you make a mistake and open a bad door? Can you notice how you can always close the door again quickly? Or can you also see a special way of taming the nasties? How will you mark the bad doors so that you will know them next time?

9. What kinds of adventures will you have when you open doors that are neither all good nor all bad, but are very interesting and exciting?

10. How will people in the palace discover that you have become their ruler by mastering the rules of possibility and understanding how the doors work? What will you do during the rest of your day or rule? Will the people cheer you as you leave at the end of the day?

11. How will you tell the story of your successes at the palace.

General Note: *This is a more advanced picturing, drawing on imagining skills developed in earlier work. Imagination also creates nightmares and horrors. The palace provides a safe frame in which to explore and work with this darker side of imagination as well as with the positive – the strength of the keys and the doors and the locks and the safety of the main part of the palace can be emphasized with young children. Comparing notes, discussing and telling some of the different stories imaginations are telling between stages can work well and will illustrate the very many possibilities.*

Story skills: *Learning to work with all sides of the imagination, not just the pleasant, is an essential part of story skill. The palace and the exploration and conquering of it gives a plot that can be developed in many different ways. Any work of fiction is, in a sense, a palace of possibility to its author at the outset – though necessarily many doors are ignored or kept locked.*

Interesting: *Understanding something of the 'dark side' of imagination is also a vital life skill. Remarks above will also point to an effective use of this picturing to develop degrees of control of some negative imaginings – though it's worth adding the caveat that working with the severely traumatized requires additional special training and knowledge.*

13. STRANGE LANDS AND PECULIAR PEOPLES

Scenario: You will visit a land that is quite different from your own land, where people look and speak and behave differently and wear entirely different clothes. They may even be from different planets or from different ages. However, they are quite friendly and allow you to walk around amongst them and watch what they are doing, so that you are able to notice ways they are acting and talking that seem quite familiar – familiar enough to make good guesses as to what they are saying, even though you do not understand any words. You can see the very different life in this land, watch strange happenings. You can even make notes or film it all before you travel home.

Stages:

1. How do you travel to this land? Will you use the Fantasy Steed or a magic carpet or simply imagine your way there?

2. As you arrive in this land and what sort of things do you notice about the people first? Are their buildings (or whatever they live in) very different? Are there streets and shops and markets or do things work very differently? What sorts of colours can you see and do you notice any unusual scents? How do you feel about being in this land?

3. You can watch some of the people quite closely. What are they doing and in what ways can you understand what they are saying?

4. Something exciting is happening. You can tell that by the way the people are acting. Do you notice their expressions and the gestures they are making? But what is the exciting thing they and you will watch now?

5. What happens next? Do you go somewhere you hadn't expected to go and see something else you hadn't expected to see? Is there an adventure?

6. Can you make some notes about things you want to tell other people about the land and the people? If you like, you can film it or draw imaginary pictures in your mind.

7. How will you tell the story of this adventure? How will you make it clear to your listeners or readers that the place and the people were so very different?

General note: This plot is very much a staple of modern children's fiction – the widely used Oxford reading scheme replays it in several forms using a magic key that takes children through time. There are many adult treatments too, ranging from science fiction to the Arabian Nights. The picturing makes a good tall story to tell in one of the Book 1 Tall Tale Telling *games and works particularly well with No. 24* Fantasy Islands and Strange Planets *– the fantasy* *steed (or whatever) can carry pictures to a series of lands or planets. I Witness (No.19 from this book) will also work well with this. Storytellers can be encouraged to explain as clearly as possible in words in what ways they understood without words for example.*

Story Skills: *Creating and imagining a fantasy land is another fiction skill. Noticing non verbal behavioural clues and finding ways to report and describe them as part of the story can be stressed. Writers often describe gestures, postures etc. as ways of conveying character, communication etc. There are many opportunities in the stages of the picturing for reinforcing ideas about description and way of creating strange effects - colour reversals, weird sounds, peculiar shapes and so on.*

Interesting: *The picturing encourages close, sympathetic observation and the development of rapport with people without words. This mirrors (and can be used to develop) another vital life skill. Going to such a place in imagination can also be used to develop confidence and social poise.*

14. THE BITE OF THE DRAGON

Scenario: You have now become a hero or heroine. You are hence able to go through an ordeal (such as being bitten by a dragon) in order to achieve an end (getting a treasure/ magic potion/ power, rescuing a person/people in distress etc.). You can take with you just one weapon/gift/special power to help, but you won't be able to avoid some pain and danger, even though you will certainly conquer and survive.

Stages:

1. You can enjoy the feeling of being a hero or heroine for a while. People like to have their champions and there's no harm in showing off a bit.

2. All champions, however, spend a while concentrating on their goals very hard, so that they are ready. You might like to imagine what the goal is today, what you are going to achieve by going through this ordeal. Maybe you can picture the thing or the power you will get or the person you will rescue. What is it going to be like when you have completed the task?

3. You will need to choose the one weapon or gift or potion etc. you are going to take with you and imagine it very clearly, noticing at least three things about it so that it will be especially powerful. Remember the rule about the pain when you do this and find a way to get ready for and deal with that in heroic style. (You can always take that relaxing Fantasy Room along in your imagination, because real heroes and heroines use it in just that way.)

4. Where will the ordeal take place and what is the painful danger you are going to face? Is it a dragon or some other kind of beast or something quite different?

5. How does the 'bite' (or whatever) happen and how will you deal with and conquer the 'biter'? How did your weapon/gift/potion etc. help?

6. Can you picture clearly the moment of victory and what it feels like to have completed the task?

7. Going back through what you have just been through, how will you tell the story to someone else, so that they can get a real feel for the ordeal?

General note: As a prelude, a discussion and listing of possible ordeals is useful. How do heroines and heroes come through the ordeals? What sorts of qualities would they have? How important is their vision of the goal in helping them through? How might powers/weapons/skills be used to make the ordeal more bearable. Ordeals, objectives and weapons can all be much more mundane and 'real world' than the examples in the outline. There is plenty of scope for adaptation to age and taste and once again, the setting can be updated and made very contemporary. The I Witness game (No.19) is good for developing the picturing into a story, which can also be made an episode in a longer quest story.

Story skills: Nothing makes a story more unbelievable than a narration which lacks any sense of the sufferings of the characters involved. A writer or storyteller needs to be able to understand what his/her characters go through as well as to view it from the outside. This picturing exercises this mental skill. Stories coming out of this visualization can be particularly vivid in the ways feelings are described.

Interesting: *This kind of metaphor can be used to overcome actual fears and to face real pain. For example, one hospice nurse uses something quite similar to help children overcome their discomfort and apprehension at blood transfusions. The story can be about the 'dragon' (or whatever), at the same time inspiring ways of dealing with the fear/pain etc., hence the suggestion of the use of the Fantasy Room in the stages. Parents may find this a useful technique and it is not without a similar relevance in some school sessions.*

15. THE ENCHANTING GARDENS

Scenario: There is a path to be followed through an enchanted and enchanting garden. Sometimes the path may be very clear, sometimes fuzzy and vague, but it will always be there. However, the garden is very attractive in all sorts of ways and there are very many marvels to enjoy, all sorts of tempting treasures. You are looking for something very important – perhaps *The Water of Life* or *Heart's Desire (see Nos. 18 & 24)*. If you leave the path, you will very probably be lost and under a spell. You might become a flower or a fountain and you won't get what you came for.

Stages:

1. How do you reach this garden? Do you go up the Golden Staircase and through the Magic door or fly there on the magic carpet? Will you enter through magnificent main gates or climb over a wall or crawl in via a tunnel or a cave? How does the path look and what sort of feelings does it give you?

2. What are you aiming to find in this garden? You can remember how important this is.

3. What is the sensation of walking along that path? What kinds of wonders do you notice first? Are the colours vivid? Can you smell flowers and hear birds singing? What else do you notice as you pass by?

4. There is something in the garden that seems to pull as a magnet pulls. It is very very attractive, but it is not what you came for. What is it and how do you resist that pull?

5. What happens when the path goes vague? How do you make it come clear again?

6. How and where do you find what you came for? Does it look as wonderful as the tempting garden or more ordinary? How do you take it and escape from the garden?

7. How will you tell the story of this adventure?

General note: Another recurring motif in fairy tale and myth. Sometimes the heroine or hero is looking for the Water of Life, sometimes for the Mirror of Truth and sometimes for something else, but there are usually the possible distractions, the need to stay on the path or something similar and the superior goal to be achieved. The picturing needs quite a lot of space for the imagining to happen and perhaps some extra hints, clues and suggestions. The Enchanting Garden can be used alone or woven in a quest tale, as suggested in Heart's Desire (p.50).

Story skills: Listing fabulous and alluring wonders is an oral storytelling elaboration skill with various practical purposes, as explained in Book 3. Spinning the Yarn. Here it clearly makes the subsequent story (told or written) work in a much more vivid way if the wonders of the enchanting garden can be seen in the picturing and described in the telling, probably using the familiar pattern of three details etc. developed in other games.

Interesting: The Enchanting Garden can be a metaphor for very many activities and processes in life which require a registering of possibilities but a central focusing on a goal and ability to ignore distractions. Passing through this magical garden can be used to symbolically rehearse such a task and achievement and to imaginatively rehearse success.

16. THE MOUNTAINS OF MISFORTUNE

Scenario: To complete your quest or journey and reach your goal, you have to get beyond the Mountains of Misfortune through a high pass. There is spell on this pass so that it will seem to you as you go through it that there are all kinds of nightmare dangers and terrible misfortunes. These may be the conventional dragons and ghouls and giants and witches and monsters and being turned to stone, or they may be much more ordinary looking but particularly scary to you. None of them will be real, but they will seem real. As long as you stay on the path, you are completely safe and they will simply vanish as you go past them. If you leave the path, you may be lost in dangerous lands or even frozen into a statue or turned into a tree.

Stages:

1. What do the mountains look like as you approach them? How do you feel about going through the pass? How important is that goal beyond the mountains right now?

2. As you start to walk up the path, what kinds of things do you notice? Is it easy to walk up the rocky path?

3. What are the first smaller dangers you see and how do you get past them and make them vanish? Do you notice how this gives you the confidence to go on further?

4. The nightmare dangers may become much more scary. What is the worst danger that might appear as you go over the mountains?... And what does it feel like when it simply vanishes?

5. As you get used to the way this path works, you could even enjoy watching dangers approaching. Can you see any more dangers and threats and notice how they disappear?

6. What is it like getting over and through that strange mountain pass and what will you find beyond it?

7. How will you tell the story of this adventure?

General Note: *Another version of the previous picturing in which there are dangers instead of wonders and attractive things. In tradition, these may combine so that there are sometimes wonders and sometimes dangers – it's possible to combine the two in another picturing, perhaps focusing on, say, a Spellbinding Forest. Although the wording suggests that the picturing is part of a quest or other larger story, the adventure can stand alone. Some of the questions and suggestions in* No.14 The Bite of the Dragon *could be added here; another possibility is to combine the illusory terrors of this picturing with 'real' ones like the dragon's bite.*

Story Skills: *This is again good preparation for handling similar episodes in traditional stories, this time allowing the storyteller to develop lists of horrors and find ways to describe them. Principles of description developed in* Book 3 Spinning the Yarn *and patterns of three features etc. are again useful. Note that an episode like this makes a good middle to a story, which only needs the addition of a beginning and an end to make the kind of complete basic plot usually taught to children in their own story making.*

Interesting: *Similar remarks as those made for The Enchanting Garden apply – many tasks in life involve conquering fears. which frequently turn out to have been based on illusions, so that this makes a good fantasy rehearsal for achievement. Children can benefit by making the 'horrors' of the mountain very much like their own fears, whilst the safety of the path is stressed.*

17. THE GALLERY OF LIVING PICTURES

Scenario: You can visit a very special gallery in a high and secret tower. This tower has previously been forbidden to you but now you have a bunch of keys to open all of its doors. Beyond the outer door, inside the tower, there are stairs with more doors at the top of each flight. When you open the last one of these doors, you'll be in the gallery where there are at least three pictures. These are living pictures of strange and fantastical places or people. You will be able to see and not be seen. You can go into the pictures if you want to or just stand outside the and look and learn in complete safety. The choice is yours.

Stages:

1. What does the key look like and how will you open that first door to show the stairs? What sort of stairs and how steep are they? How do you feel as you climb those stairs and open the second door?

2. Is the next flight of stairs different or the same? Is it easy to open the third door and go up the next flight? Does the third door look and feel different? What kinds of sounds do you hear as you open it? What is the smell of the place? Is there another flight of stairs and another door?

3. When you open the final door, how soon do you see the full gallery with the pictures? How big is it and how is it lit? Is it cold or warm? What sort of furniture is there (if any)?

4. How do you notice the pictures and what kinds of frames do they have? You may be able to see into the pictures straight away or perhaps there are curtains or veils to draw back.

5. In the first picture, if you look hard you'll be able to see or sense in some other way a whole landscape of some kind. It could be a country scene or in a city, in a hot or a cold land, near the sea or far inland. But it is definitely strange in some way. How?

6. In the second one somewhere, you could spot the kind of person who could help you in all sorts of ways. It could be a wizard or a fairy or a good genie or a spirit of some kind. Can you watch and learn some skills and tricks or even talk to and make friends with this being?

7. You may not want to spend too long looking at the third picture, but remember you are in a very safe place here. In the picture is some dangerous creature – a dragon or a monster or a ghost or whatever. Again you can watch and learn about their weak spots.

8. Perhaps you would like to go into just one of the pictures to fetch a treasure

or learn something very important, or perhaps you would prefer to tiptoe out and go back down the stairs again.

9. How will you tell the story to someone else so that they will know how much you have learned?

General Note: The keys and the very many possibilities in the pictures invite comparison with The Palace of Possibility *(No.12), but the gallery is still more advanced since it allows picturers to stand outside the imagining and observe it. The picturing can be done in a wide variety of different ways. It does not have to centre on traditional fantasy as suggested here and what is in the pictures can be left open or given different limitations. As in* The Golden Staircase & the Magic Door *(No.2), it's not necessary to use the staircase imagery if this is not appropriate – the main point is to have something that a person can progress along by gentle stages, which allows imagining to develop gradually. There are various stories in folklore that use this kind of image.*

Story Skills: The skill of both standing outside the 'picture' and entering into it is a mental skill in story work. Also the structure of the visualization gives a plot that works by itself in a simple form, whilst having a potential as the start of (say) a more complex quest tale, perhaps developed through the scheme in Hearts Desire *(No.24).*

Interesting: Although this is done for creative fun here, it's again useful to be aware of the fact that it resembles procedures used by therapists using the imaginative mind to work with difficult and sometimes traumatic experiences. A skilled therapist would emphasize the safety of the 'gallery' (or equivalent) and stress the curtains initially to increase the comfort and control, avoiding any suggestion that pictures could be entered at the initial stage.

18. THE WATER OF LIFE

Scenario: The Water of Life is often sought in stories and with good reason, since it can heal the sick and give back life to the weary and the dying. One drop of the water of life placed in a fountain will become a marvellous torrent, always renewing itself. Why not find the water of life for yourself or to help someone else?

Stages:

1. Since the Water of Life is not found just anywhere, where will you seek it? Some look in marvellous gardens, some in the mountains or in caves or in far away palaces or the lairs of wizards. Others have other ideas. How will you travel to the Water of Life? Will you use a magic carpet or a fantasy steed or Cloud 9?

2. What kinds of adventures did you have in finding the mythical water? Did you pass through ordeals like *The Bite of the Dragon* (p.33), find your way through *The Mountains of Misfortune* (p.34) and into *The Enchanting Garden* (p.33)? Did it take a long time or a short time? Did you have companions and helpers on the journey or did you go alone? You can look back through your journey to this place now and think about how all those adventures have made you a true hero or heroine.

3. Finding the Water of Life may be a little different from the way you imagined it. How do you imagine it?......

4. Where will you actually find it? What will it look like? Does the light make patterns on it? Does it smell good? What kind of container will you use to carry some of it away?

5. How does it feel when you very carefully taste a just a little of it yourself? How does its marvellous power begin to work on you and give you new strength?

6. Will you have more adventures and difficulties in carrying the container back? What kinds of adventures might those be? Or perhaps there seems to be any easy route.

7. What is it like when you place some of that water in a dry fountain at home and it suddenly becomes a marvellous torrent? Can you watch that for a moment? Are there particular things you would like to see the water do?

8. How will you tell the story of this adventure from start to finish?

General Note: *In this last picturing, a traditional symbol used in many fairy tales and legends has been chosen as an example of one goal storytellers could be aiming to reach in earlier games or perhaps in a quest such as* Heart's Desire *at the end of Part 2. The stages suggest linking various games to make a long story – though these suggestions can be taken out if the picturing is to be used alone. Unlike adults past a certain age, some children may need a little convincing that this special water is worth the trouble, but since it can be a very strong sensory image, it usually 'takes' with some persuasion and vivid imagining. Children can also be allowed to give the water additional miraculous powers.*

Story Skills: *Again turning the picturing into words develops imaginative and verbal control, whilst making the full story as implied here involves handling what could be called a natural plot – quests have an episodic form that matches many children's early attempts at longer narrative. This quest can be given a complexity and balance through the different picturings.*

Interesting: *Picturing the miraculous water in vivid multi-sensory ways and imagining how it can heal can again have some very real effects, assisting actual healing in the same way that many placebos trick the immune system. The Water of Life can be a good picturing for children and adults going through surgery etc. as well as other difficulties requiring forms of emotional healing.*

PART 2. TELL IT ON

This section includes six lively games for complementing the picturings and developing them as stories in oral games. Games in the other booklets can also be used for this purpose, particularly games from Book 1. Tall Tale Telling – each visualization can be treated as a tall tale and the various ways of questioning and developing the story given there can be used to spin the spoken story. There are also all kinds of other ways of achieving the same effect in story making, storytelling, drama etc.

19. I WITNESS

Group game. Also pairs & small groups.

The 'storyteller' is chosen. S/he has 'seen' imaginary or fantastical things through one of the picturings and is asked about this by the group or partner. Questioners are encouraged to be curious, not sceptical – to ask about the kind of natural detail a person who has been to, say, a Miracle Market or a Castle in the Air would be likely to know. The storyteller is encouraged to check his/her answers by recalling (or extending) the picturing - by looking at, sensing, hearing etc. the details asked for, rather than saying the first thing that comes to mind. There will usually be a set number of questions, say 5 or 7.

To develop the questioning as the game becomes familiar, group members can be encouraged to think about different senses involved in the picturing and to ask questions around them, to find out how the storyteller's experience may differ from their own. Questioners may also ask about specific parts of the picturing they themselves recall.

General note: *This is very like the questioning games in* Book 1. Tall Tale Telling. *It may take a while to get past the glib and facile response and get storytellers to make use of picturing ability to check and develop their answers, though some do this naturally. Again if the group (or person) knows a game like* Fantastic Fibs *(Book 1. No.1) , they will need schooling in less aggressive and more encouraging questioning.*

Story Skills: *Combining the 'seeing' involved in the picturing with the 'reality testing' of the questions mimics the mental processes of writers and storytellers, who constantly ask themselves questions about how to 'make the story true' at the same time as consulting imagination. And in order to make a story happen 'out there' on the page or in shared words, a process of explanation has to happen – narrative is, in an important sense, explanation. The game develops imaginative and verbal fluency.*

Interesting: *Because you can imagine a thing, this doesn't mean that it is therefore either true or realistic. Yet good imagining balanced by realism helps to open up perception of the many possibilities in life. Encouraging the use of questioning along with imagining is not simply an exercise in story making; it is a rehearsal for effective ways of shaping a life.*

20. WHISPERINGS

Pairs

This is a telling game in pairs for use following any of the picturings. Partner A tells Partner B the story of what s/he 'saw', giving as many details as possible. Partner B can prompt with questions as in the *I Witness* game above and must try to find out as much as possible. S/he must listen closely and mentally record what is told. Once the 'story' is complete, Partner B tells the story and Partner A listens etc. They must do all this in secret and in low whispering voices, as if exchanging confidences. This has an important purpose if a game like *Terrible Trials* (No.22) or *Heart's Desire* (No.24) follows on so that listeners become referees, though is a good listening exercise in itself and gives the game an interesting 'flavour'.

To develop this skill of listening closely and being able to recall what has been heard, a variation on the *Pass it On* game (Book 1. No.2) can be used. Participants will change partners and will describe not what they 'saw' but parts of the 'secret' the other person told them – again as if sharing a secret not all should know. This is told as a third person narrative about 'this person I know'. This can be made particularly interesting if the second partner doesn't know the identity of the teller's first partner. (This can be engineered for example by using two working spaces. The two halves of the group are paired for the first part of the exercise in separate places, so that Group A doesn't know how Group B was paired.) In this case, the teller disguises the identity of the person who told the 'secret' and tells a tale of what this person (boy/girl/man/woman) told him/her. The listener(s) might then guess who the original teller was.

If storytellers passing on 'stories' think that some parts of what they relay may embarrass the original tellers, they are encouraged to edit or to make up alternatives. Since this is a storytelling exercise, they are also free to make up what they can't remember.

General Note: The game can be played without the Pass it On *stage. Equally the* Pass it On *exercise can be extended as suggested in Book 1, so that the 'story' is passed on several times, changing naturally as it does so. The 'story' is then told back to the group and (perhaps) compared with the original teller's experience. The game also encourages less confident and 'loud' tellers to develop speaking and listening skills.*

Story Skills: At the first stage, tellers are again putting into spoken words what they have only imagined so far - an essential story skill. Some of the picturings suggest an outline plot, which is being developed through the interaction – and through the Pass it On *stage. Listening closely and then retelling the other person's experience as a story gives another kinds of experience of working with a received plot.*

Interesting: *The game can also be used to encourage sensitivity and empathy, particularly if the picturing is very personal as for example* The Fantasy Room *(No.1) might be. How much of a person's 'secret' can you tell without betraying that person? How well did you listen to the teller? This use of the game requires a little adaptation so that the embarrassment rule is stressed during the re-telling, whilst during the earlier picturing, listeners could be encouraged to make the pictures as very personal metaphors.*

21. HEROES, HEROINES AND FOOLS

Storytellers must tell a story based on the picturing about a person (not themselves) who (for example) once floated on a magic cloud or flew on a magic carpet and went to a castle in the air. In a group situation, the group leader might award a point for each part of the original visualization(s) worked into the narrative – but two points for extra embellishments that enhance the telling. At the early stage, questions can be asked as in *I Witness* (No.19) or as in *Fantastic Fibs* (Book 1. No 1); as the game becomes familiar, storytellers are encouraged just to tell. As an incentive with children, the telling can be timed – the longer it lasts the better, so that the champion teller is the one who spins out the narrative longest.

The game can be played in pairs (with or without the questioning) to develop a tale that will eventually be told to the group. Partner A tells and Partner B listens, then they change round. Next they change partners and swap stories again, telling the same story again, but adding to it as much as possible, so that they will have long tales to tell to the group eventually. Partners can be swapped several times in group situations. Or after (say) three partner changes, groups of four exchange tales to encourage speaking to larger groups.

General Note: *The third person narrative called for here will probably naturally have been preceded by a first person narrative stage, in which storytellers make up stories coming out of the picturing with themselves as heroes and heroines. This is, of course, suggested in notes on the picturings. A stage of picturing and describing the person to whom the adventures will happen can be introduced, perhaps with a storytelling game like* My Friend Boogle *(No.18 from Book 1). As implied by the title of this game, the central character can be treated very seriously or with humour.*

Story Skills: *Converting first person experience to third person narrative is basic to fiction of all kinds. Storytellers can be encouraged to draw on the plot suggestions that go with many of the picturings – the three adventures that should connect with three gifts or three helpers for example, or the miracles one might expect after a visit to* The Miracle Market *(No.11) or from* The Water of Life *(No 18).*

Interesting: *Changing any story from first person to third makes the storyteller more objective, takes him or her into a stance of looking from outside the experience. This is made use of in various forms of Narrative Therapy.*

22. TERRIBLE TRIALS

This game is to be played by a group following picturings such as *Three Magic Gifts* (No.5) or *Three Magic Helpers* (No.6) or even *The Water of Life* (No. 18). Any of these and other picturings may already have been combined with *Cloud 9* (No 3), *The Castle in the Air* (No.4) and/or *The Miracle Market* (No.11). In a formal workshop setting, these will usually have been followed by at least the first stage of *Whisperings* (No.20), so that group members will have revealed and talked about their gifts to at least one person.

The storyteller is chosen and is told that s/he is about to set off on a journey.

In the simplest version, this will be simply returning home from the place in which the gifts were received or the miracles were purchased. If s/he gets back safely with all three gifts (etc.) intact, those gifts become permanent, so that each can be used again and again. But on the journey, each gift can only be used once; a second use means that the gift will be lost after that use.

The storyteller does not reveal the nature of the gift to the group. The person (or people) who heard the story in *Whisperings* also keeps the secret, but now becomes the referee(s), so that the storyteller is prevented from making up a completely new gift not already described during the game. The rest of the group will then present and describe to the storyteller successively three terrible trials. The nature of these will vary with the age and taste of the group. In a fantasy setting, the trials might be monsters or dragons, seas of fire, wizards and witches and so on. In a sophisticated adult version, the trials could be losing confidence or the power of thinking clearly (see also *Use It or Lose It* No 23), whilst of course there are many ways those two levels can be combined. To prevent the trials becoming too severe, each must be described in three 'strokes' – the dragon breathes fire, is a mile high and its breath is also poisonous for example.

The usual procedure in an oral group game is for the storyteller to firstly describe his/her exit and first mode of travel from the castle/market/palace etc. where the gifts (or whatever) were received. The first unexpected trial is then given by the group – in the case of children, the class or group might put up their hands and offer trials, the best (or worst) or which is chosen by the teacher/group leader/parent. Or trials are first invented in a separate story making exercise. The storyteller describes how s/he deals with this, using either sheer cunning or one of the magic gifts to do so. Now the group offer the second challenge and again the storyteller responds and so on through the third trial, providing that the storyteller has come through the previous trials.

Finally, the story is re-told by the storyteller or by the leader, with the help of the group, as a story about the storyteller, using his/her first name.

General Note: *As suggested above, there are many ways to vary and adapt this game. It can also be used as part of the quest in* Hearts Desire *(No. 24). The trials can be limited in various other ways, for example by setting a range of trial types as in* Hazards & Challenges *(Book 1. No.7). The two games are very similar and depend on the same kind of inventiveness and improvisation encouraged throughout Book 1, but the storyteller can be even more successful in coping with the challenges because the 'gifts' have been seen and held etc. in advance through the picturing, which also gives more of a plot with which to conjure a tale.* Terrible Trials *can be made to work with many of the picturings not mentioned above.*

Story Skills: *The 'serendipity principle' comes into play again – storytellers would probably not have included the trials they are given, but must draw on their imagining and storytelling ability to survive and complete the game. The trials will extend their narrative to make a longer story that can be re-told or written. Hence the game also illustrates the principle of introducing difficulties to strengthen a narrative*

Interesting: *This game encourages quick thinking and adaptability, as well as confidence. The more adult version of the trials mentioned above clearly has possibilities in therapeutic settings, but this is also true of the fantasy imagery children enjoy: a terrible trial can be introduced because it naturally symbolizes a challenge the child will face. The victory can hence be emotionally loaded.*

23. USE IT OR LOSE IT

The storyteller has gained something through one of the picturings. It could be magic gifts, magic helpers, the ability to float on Cloud 9 or go into a fantasy room; it might be a magic carpet or the Water of Life – anything in fact suggested by any picturing. S/he returns to the ordinary world. How does s/he use the secret gift/experience etc. to change things? What kind of successes and failures will s/he have?

The storyteller is chosen and explains the first gift or helper or whatever and how s/he will use it – perhaps s/he has a healing potion or a purse of gold that is never empty. Members of the group or the partner now ask 'what if' questions to test the 'story' and see how well it can work - *'What if you heal too many people so that doctors and nurses are out of work?'* ... *'What if everyone wants to steal your magic purse?'*... *'What if you spend too much time in your fantasy room?'* etc. Questions can be limited to a set number per gift/experience. The storyteller answers each question, explaining what s/he will do to change things in that circumstance.

After answering the set questions, the storyteller has a story (or potential story) set in every day circumstance in which s/he uses the fantasy gift/experience etc. in various ways and meets various challenges. This can be further developed in telling and/or writing. It might remain a first person narrative or become the kind of third person tale explored above in No. 21 *Heroes, Heroines & Fools*

General note: *The basic game suggests only uses and successes, but the danger of losing the gift if the storyteller cannot use it in some way in solving the difficulty can be introduced to give the game an edge. Compare this game with* Wishes Three *in Book 4. New Lamps for Old.*

Story Skills: *Fantasy is not enough to make a story. The fantasy has to be tested through 'real world' events. This game combines fantasy and every day reality, which can stretch the basic imagining done in the picturing to make a plot of real interest.*

Interesting: *The procedure in this game gives the chance to take imaginings already described as (say) confidence enhancing (for example, No.6* Three Magic Helpers *or No.14* The Bite of the Dragon*) and to test them against real life in imagination. This can strengthen the changes made through imagination and prepare the ability to cope with setbacks.*

24. HEART'S DESIRE

This extended game allows various picturings and storytelling games to be combined to make a long quest story. It's a good example of how to integrate the various techniques in the book in story work, though there are many other ways to do this.

Scenario: Storytellers (all participants) will go on a quest to find their heart's desire. As in myth and legend, this is supposed to be what they truly and most deeply desire. (In a fun story workshop, this doesn't need to be taken too seriously and can be done as pure fantasy.) The first stage is to picture the heart's desire represented as an image – a chalice or a chest, a golden fleece, the Water of Life or whatever. Participants will need an image that feels really attractive, so it's worth encouraging them to spend time on this, getting a clear sense of something that feels right. They will set out on a quest through the game to attain this.

Stages:

As part of the stages of the game, various picturings can be introduced, invoked or re-visited. Here is one scheme by way of example, though it should be easy to invent others.

1. Spending time in *The Fantasy Room* (No.1) or any other imaginary place that is really relaxing and soothing, allowing the Heart's Desire image to develop. (Clues and cues and suggestions can be given after a time.)
2. Going up the staircases (etc.) to *The Gallery of Living Pictures* (No 17).
3. Finding *Three Magic Gifts* (No. 5) or Three Magic Helpers (No. 6) through one of the pictures in the gallery.
4. Seeing some dangers ahead through a second picture and developing the courage and skill to deal with them, maybe by entering the picture and doing *The Bite of the Dragon* picturing (No.14), through which an extra gift representing the courage required could be attained.

5. Seeing the route to Heart's Desire through the third picture and setting out on the journey through entering that picture, perhaps taming a *Fantasy Steed* (as in No.7) to ride in the process.

6. *Terrible Trials* – encountering at least three trials on the journey to Heart's Desire, supplied through the story game (No.22), or introduced through *The Enchanting Garden* (No.15) or *Mountains of Misfortune (*No.16).

7. Arriving at and attaining the Heart's Desire.

8. Telling the story.

Each stage can be approached through picturing and through storytelling as in other games and exercises. Stages can be built up over several sessions or done more briefly in one or two sessions.

General note: *This example scheme is quite complicated. It's possible to be a lot simpler, linking only two or three picturings and/or games. It's also possible to get much more complicated by integrating more (and even all) of the games and picturings; the scope is extensive. As a final stage, a group can create a shared quest tale about a hero or heroine (or both) in which the kinds of adventures in the scheme above might feature.*

Story Skills: *All extended narratives are composed of smaller episodes joined together with greater of lesser success. The quest tale developing out of* Heart's Desire *is very flexible, allowing episodes to be bolted on or dumped according to necessity. However, the theme allows for some more serious and fundamental elements of meaningful fiction to show through and develop naturally.*

Interesting: *The traditional quest is also a psychological and emotional journey. There are many opportunities in this scheme for making personal discoveries and changes.*

ABOUT THE AUTHOR

For more than two decades, Rob Parkinson has told his tales in all kinds of places, from theatres, festivals, schools and libraries to pubs and clubs and restaurants and zoos and even shacks in the Australian outback. A varied career path prior to becoming a professional storyteller included teaching, driving trucks and taxis, restoring antiques, playing guitar in bars, painting signs and travelling extensively – and provided vital experience to draw on as a tale teller. He has chaired the Society for Storytelling, run a story club and appeared in front on millions of television viewers reciting Chaucer's tales and playing some of his ancient instruments. His unique fantasy songs for children have continued to prove enormously popular across a broad age range.

In recent years, Rob has focused his attention on the uses of stories in education, therapy, counselling and communication in general. In addition to his work as as a tale teller, he now has successful practice as a therapist and runs training courses for professionals in all walks of life. He has published numerous articles and papers on storytelling and is the author of Lantern of Imaginings - The Secrets of Change through Stories *(HG Publishing 2006).*

Imaginary Journeys *focuses on positive uses of imagination, very much including storytelling. Visit our web site to view the full range we are developing or write/telephone for information.*

www.imaginaryjourneys.co.uk
27 London Road, Tonbridge, Kent TN10 3AB, UK
Tel/fax +44 (0)1732 362356